A Brief Description Of The Facilities And Advantages Which A Road Across Central America From Admiral's Bay, Or Chiriqui Lagoon, On The Atlantic, To Chiriqui Bay, On The Pacific, Would Afford To The Commerce Of The World

A BRIEF DESCRIPTION

OF THE FACILITIES AND ADVANTAGES WHICH

A ROAD

ACROSS CENTRAL AMERICA,

FROM

ADMIRAL'S BAY, OR CHIRIQUI LAGOON,

ON THE ATLANTIC, TO

CHIRIQUI BAY, ON THE PACIFIC,

WOULD AFFORD TO THE

COMMERCE OF THE WORLD.

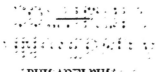

PHILADELPHIA:

B. FRANKLIN JACKSON, PRINTER,

1852.

A BRIEF DESCRIPTION

*Of the facilities and advantages which a road across
Central America from Admiral's Bay or Chiriqui
Lagoon, on the Atlantic, to Chiriqui Bay, on the
Pacific, would afford to the Commerce of the World.*

The manifest aspirations of the whole commercial
world, for improved means of communication across
the isthmus separating the Atlantic and Pacific
Oceans, have imparted a new interest, as well as a
new value to privileges of transit, mining and coloni-
zation conceded by its governments. England and
the United States have been foremost in their anxiety
for the success of such enterprises, and have even
made it a subject of international treaty to secure the
free exercise of any right of way which may be granted by the local authorities on the Isthmus to their
respective subjects for the indiscriminate benefit of
all nations. Thus, under the guarantee of two of the
most powerful nations in the world, individual enterprise, directed towards this quarter, is amply secured
against all danger, whilst the rich resources of the
country to be traversed, cannot fail to insure the most
prosperous results to those who shall establish a
communication between the Atlantic and Pacific
at a point the most accessible, and at the same time
the most healthy.

At the present moment three lines of communication have been commenced upon, to connect the Atlantic and Pacific Oceans, all of them by companies formed in the United States, and which promise more or less profits to those interested therein, so soon as they shall be completed for travel. Those routes are known as the Tehuantepec, San Juan de Nicaragua, and the Panama lines.

According to the best information to be gathered on the subject, the first of these projected lines has obstacles of a local character to encounter almost insurmountable. or which can only be vanquished by a vast outlay of means, should the government of Mexico permit the enterprise to be carried through, which is very problematical.

The San Juan de Nicaragua line, now partially open, can never be a formidable rival, the changes necessary from a land conveyance, to water carriage on the lake, and subsequent necessity for canoes to descend the rapids and rivers which lie in the course of this line, are found to be almost unsupportable for passengers, and can never be expected to compete in the transmission of merchandise.

The other projected line, via Chagres to Panama, is found to be practically inconvenient, from the insecurity of its harbor on the Atlantic, its fatal climate, and swampy nature of the country, which has only enabled those engaged thereon, after three years of enormous expenditure and loss of life, to complete the rail-road to the extent of less than one-sixth of the whole distance yet to be performed to Panama, where a wharf has also to be carried out for the enormous distance of two miles, as the shore there shelves so gradually that the steamers resorting thereto at present never approach nearer to Panama, rendering the operation of embarking and disembarking very inconvenient, tedious, and troublesome.

Intermediate, however, between the Nicaragua and Panama routes, another exists which is entirely free from the objections which, either separately or collectively, attach to the others alluded to, and where almost every facility for opening a road between the two oceans, has been bountifully supplied by the hand of nature. The route in question is from Chiriqui Lagoon, or Admiral's Bay, on the Atlantic, to Chiriqui Bay, on the Pacific. It passes through the healthy province of Chiriqui or Fabriga, in New Grenada, between the 7° and 9° of north latitude, and 81° 5 longitude west from Greenwich, being about 180 miles due west from Panama, but distant 540 miles by coast line on the Pacific. The distance from sea to sea is here only about 18 leagues, whilst the highest point in the contemplated course, above the level of the ocean, does not reach 160 feet.

Admiral's Bay on the Atlantic, and Chiriqui Bay on the Pacific, are both magnificent and safe harbors, of easy approach, whilst excellent coal, and in abundance, exists in the immediate proximity of each.

A grant or patent, in due form, for the exclusive right of way at this important point has been granted for the term of 60 years by the government of New Grenada and the provincial authorities of Chiriqui; this valuable patent, together with upwards of 40,000 acres of land, conceded therewith, can now be secured on equitable terms for an association which may desire to avail of the great advantages which it holds out for the profitable employment of capital, over every other project of a similar nature which has yet been brought before the public.

For more full information, attention is requested to the following reports of competent parties who have visited or surveyed the route in question across the Isthmus of Chiriqui.

REPORT BY WILLIAM NORRIS, Esq.*

CIVIL ENGINEER.

In accordance with my promise, I have the honor of stating, in writing, my views in regard to the projected Transit Route from the Atlantic to the Pacific, through the Province of Chiriqui, Isthmus of Panama; first, giving you a short account of the character of the country, together with other facts, founded upon personal observation.

The Chiriqui Lagoon, the terminus on the Atlantic, is a harbor, perhaps, unexcelled in the world for every good quality; and with a *healthy climate*.

SECTION 1. *Eight Miles.*—The land rises gradually from the Lagoon, until it attains a level of 14 to 15 feet above the Sea, where the Hills commence; this section is crossed by several small streams. The Forests contain all the resinous woods—the majestic

*Mr. Norris was engaged as a Chief Engineer for the Preliminary Surveys made by the Panama Rail Road Company.

Cedar and other valuable enduring woods,—the soil, rich clay, producing abundantly all the Tropical fruits.

SECTION 2. *Sixteen or Seventeen Miles.*—Through valleys slightly undulating, and over ridges, to an apparent elevation of 60 or 70 feet; this section is also covered with Forests of Cedar and other enduring woods—several mountain streams are met with, and also dry gullies. The soil here is gravel.

SECTION 3. *Five or Six Miles.*—Through valleys of the main chain of the Cordilleras, rugged and distorted but not destroying a gentle grade to the summit, which I estimate at from 150 to 160 feet above the level of the Atlantic—soil, clay and gravel.

SECTION 4. *Four Miles.*—Descending gradually towards the Pacific—slightly undulating—many gullies, but neither of width or depth—soil, sand and debris.

SECTION 5. *Twelve Miles* of Savannah, nearly a dead level to the old town of David—occasional gullies, two or three small streams; small clumps of trees—soil, gravel and debris. Primitive formation, an extinct volcanic mountain in view.

SECTION 6. *Seven Miles* to Rio " Santa Martha," where the tide ebbs and flows from 8 to 10 feet—this river, I am informed, carries 20 to 30 feet to its mouth, distant 16 miles—level throughout; soil, gravel and debris.

SECTION 7. *Eight or Nine Miles* to the Pacific coast, to the Port of David, at the mouth of the Santa Martha. In the neighborhood of the mouth of the Santa Martha, are several Islands, rich in tropical productions, and inhabited. It is said that coal has been found upon one of them.

The coast here is shelving and has safe anchorage

in three fathoms at low water, within 1900 feet of shore,—the tide rises and falls 21 to 22 feet.

In the vicinity of Section 1, good bituminous coal abounds; apparently in great quantities.

Sections 1, 2, 3, and part of 4, abound in Cedars of majestic growth, from 2 feet to 9 feet diameter, with straight stems from 40 to 90 and 100 feet. In these sections also are found in abundance, the Zapadillo and the Nisperos, both species of timber resembling the Black African oak; and of unsurpassing durability, I have seen this timber in posts and frames of houses, and in gun carriages, in the Fortress at Porto Bello, and in the Castle of San Lorenzo at Chagres. I am credibly informed that those self same posts, frames, and gun carriages, were first put into use, in 1685, A. D. I have specimens of these woods, cut from the same posts, frames and gun carriages.

In sections 2, 3, 4, and 5, the geological formations indicate an abundance of the precious metals.

When I traversed this country a few months since, I was struck with the many facilities of making a road there, from ocean to ocean; but under a supposition that the government of New Grenada had given the Panama Company a monopoly for the Isthmus, I gave up all idea of it. But now finding a "de facto" grant for this route, I have pleasure in congratulating the proprietors, upon holding a privilege far more valuable, than either the "Panama," the "San Juan de Nicaragua," or the "Tehuantepec."

My experience upon the Panama Railroad, as a Chief Engineer in the preliminary surveys, enables me to decide, with some accuracy, upon the comparative merits of the two routes, and I have no hesitation in giving the preference, even at the same cost, to the Chiriqui.

The Panama Railroad will be 47 miles in length. The Chiriqui Plank Road will be 55 to 60 miles.

The total cost of the Chiriqui, with capacity of doing same duty as the Panama, will not amount to *one fourth* of the cost of the Panama, and if care and despatch be used, the Chiriqui route, with a firm substantial Plank Road can be finished and in successful operation, before the Panama Road can possibly be completed.

Another important point in favor of the Chiriqui route is the general good health of the country. Intermittent fevers prevail only upon the banks of the rivers near the coast.

I have the honor to be, &c.

(*Signed,*) WILLIAM NORRIS,

Civil Engineer.

Philadelphia, December 1, 1851.

REPORT BY ROBERT McDOWALL, M. D.

RESIDING AT DAVID, PROVINCE OF CHIRIQUI.

Of all the provinces that constitute the Isthmus of Panama, there is none more pleasant to the eye, more valuable for its geographical position, for its agricultural capacities, and topographical superiority, than the province of Chiriqui. One of the first points of the American Continent touched at by Colon, and yet at this present day scarcely known. It has one of the finest harbors in the world, (a matter of the highest importance, especially on the Atlantic Coast of the Isthmus,) called the Admiral's Bay, on one coast, and secure roadsteads on the tranquil Pacific. It lies between 7° and 9° north latitude, and 81° 5' west longitude. Limited on the east by the province of Veraguas, north by the Atlantic, south by the Pacific, and west by Costa Rica. The Cordilleras divide it in two unequal parts, north and south. The northern, about one-third of the entire width, is the region of the Cordilleras, from the foot of the latter to the border of the Pacific, consists almost entirely of extensive plains, formed by a gradual descent of the land from the mountains, until lost in the level of the South Sea. Population is all that is required to make the desert smile like the rose. Look at those immense plains, bounded north by the majestic Andes, far off in the distance, below the twinkling Polar Star on the one hand, and the great Southern Sea, stretching away towards the coast of " Rich Cathay" on the other; covered only by grazing cattle, with little or no cultivation, though from the oak region of the Cordilleras, down to the mangroves on the sea side, the industrious farmer could select just exactly the soil and temperature he requires. To one who has seen the old world with its overburthened population, a population of industrious moral families, who ask no other favor from God and their fellow men, than permission to "earn their bread by the sweat of their brow," he would feel, I say, that it is a pity so much fine land, and so accessible, should be barren, for want of hands to accept the bounty so freely offered. How many cold shivering human beings could become happy here! where only wander

undomesticated cattle, that produce neither milk nor
cheese!! Here it would puzzle a well man to die of
hunger. The cow and the plantain tree feed the poor
native, almost without any care on his part, and if his
thatched hut does not leak, he merrily bids "dull care
begone."

The population of this province is about 20,000.
David is the principal town—Dolega, Alange, Gualaca,
Los Remedios, Tole, and one or two small villages are
not of such importance—the first, Dolega, about a
league from David, nearer the Cordilleras, is remark-
able for the longevity of its inhabitants, many of whom
have lived more than a century. The life and customs
of the original inhabitants is simple and pastoral, whose
uniform tenor is only broken occasionally by the pro-
cessions and feast days of the Church, their religion
being purely Roman Catholic.

There are five races of Indians that inhabit the
mountainous regions bordering upon the Atlantic, from
Bocas del Toro, to Cape Gracias a Dios; these different
tribes are known by the names of Caribes, Mosquitos,
Blancos, Valientes, and Guaimies; these last are most
known, as they are in the habit of visiting the towns
of the province to exchange fishing nets, bags, resins,
sarsaparilla, &c., for common calico, drills, &c., to make
clothing for their families. On the discovery of America the Indians had gold in abundance, but now such
is the horror that the traditions of their fathers have
inspired against this metal, so fatal and destructive to
their race, that no consideration will tempt them to
touch, or give the least information to a white man
about their ancient mines. These Indians invariably
inhabit what are called the "tierras baldias," or gov-

ernment lands. They seldom or never make their
towns in the plains.

The principal products of the province are Indian
corn, rice, and dried beef, the greater part of which is
sent to Panama. The mode of preparing the land is
by burning, similar to that used on the Coast of Africa,
a mode not only defective in itself, but ruinous to the
best timber of the country. Cocoa and coffee produce
very abundantly, and the quality of the sugar, made
without the least knowledge of refining, speaks greatly
in favor of the soil and the sugar cane; cotton also,
of good staple and quality, the caoutchouc tree abounds
on the coasts of both oceans; sarsaparilla, croton and
castor oil, balsams of copaiba, and peru, with many
other valuable medicinal plants abound in the forests;
palm oil, with the aid of a press, could be exported in
considerable abundance. The mountains besides afford
very rare and curious plants of the orchidean family,
including the fragrant vanilla, and bignonia; all of
which could be easily shipped to order, to supply the
increasing wants of intellectual luxury.

A few analytical experiments on a small scale have
shown the mineralogical constitution of the country to
be no less interesting. Coal of a good quality is found
on one of the islands, "Muerto," near the port on this
side. We have evidences of the existence in more or
less abundance, of platina, gold, nickle, tin, vanadium,
barium, and other rare metals, one of which seems to
be new, differing from all the known habitudes of other
metals; it seems, however, to have been known to
the ancient Indians, as we find in their graves alloys
of this metal, with copper, in the form of bats, frogs,
&c., quite unoxidated; it resists acids for some length

of time, has almost the color and specific gravity of gold itself. For domestic and other utensils it would be far more eligible than all the hitherto compositions in imitation of silver; united with lead it makes an excellent drawing pencil.

What is most essential then to make available all these untroubled riches? First, *a Road* that shall open up intercourse between these fine plains and the Atlantic. Secondly—Inhabitants to make use of the vast acres of unoccupied lands. For these great benefits the people of this generation look to your philanthropy, energy, and enterprising genius. All are anxiously awaiting the result of the Road privilege now in your possession.

R. McDOWALL, M. D.

DAVID, 15th April, 1852.

REPORT OF JOHN WHITING, Esq.,

CIVIL ENGINEER OF DAVID, PROVINCE OF CHIRIQUI.

The Isthmus, at Chiriqui, was formerly part of the Province of Veraguas, bounded on the west by the Republic of Costa Rica, in Central America, but has lately been erected into an independent department, and named Chiriqui. David is the Capitol; the Legislature meets there annually, and it is the residence of the Governor. In the town and surrounding vicinity there are about 4000 inhabitants, the province containing in all about 25,000; the climate is healthy in the extreme. There are no low and marshy lands here like those on the Chagres and Panama route; the table-lands and plains are continually ventilated and refreshed by the strong breezes from the north. There is no effluvium or miasmatic malaria to be found from the decomposed vegetation to endanger health. It is the finest part of the Isthmus, equally adapted for agriculture, or for raising cattle; vegetation is so rapid that several crops could be raised with ease, annually. The productions are innumerable: maize, coffee, tobacco, cotton, rice, yams, yucas, sugar cane, potatoes and sweet potatoes, with all the tropical fruits, plantains, bananas, oranges, lemons, grapes, olives, &c. The soil is not only capable of producing tropical grains, fruits and vegetables, but also nearly all the northern productions; in the high lands near the Cordilleras of Bocas del Toro, the climate is well adapted for them; on the plains from the base of the mountains to the shores of the Pacific Ocean innumerable herds of the finest cattle are raised—there are also many curious and useful plants, gums and resins, the canchalagua, sarsaparilla, cedron, gutta percha, caoutchouc, senna, vanilla, and Tonquin beans, &c., also dye-woods of every class and color, with many fine, valuable timbers, such as mahogany, rose-wood, cedar, and oak in the high lands. The mineral resources of the country are very abundant, gold, silver, copper, iron, lead, quicksilver, &c. Many of these mines can be profitably and easily worked when accessible.

The commercial and agricultural state of this highly favored country, where nature has spread her choicest gifts with an unsparing hand, remains yet to be developed. The only trade being between David and Panama, where some small craft ply, laden with the products of the country, which meet with a ready sale for the California Steamers; a considerable number of cattle are also driven down to Panama for the same consumption; the greater number, however, are killed and made into jerked beef, for more distant markets, where it meets with ready sale, at handsome profits.

✔ All that is wanting, however, are good roads, and easy communication from Ocean to Ocean. For this purpose an exclusive grant has been given by the Provincial Authorities; the distance is only eighteen leagues; full two-thirds of the distance is a level plain; the route has been explored, and no difficulty or obstacle has been encountered which cannot be easily surmounted. On the Atlantic side there is the beautiful Bay of Bocas del Toro or Admiral's, second to none in the world for capacity and safety; it is completely closed in and safe from gales and storms. There is room enough and sufficient water to accommodate all the navies of the commercial world. On the Pacific there is a safe and commodious harbor at Chiriqui Bay. Once open this great and important route, and a change will come over the scene; not only will the productions of this province be increased an hundred fold, but the productions of the neighboring province of Veraguas, equally rich as that of Chiriqui, would take advantage of this great improvement, and an extensive and lucrative trade must pour into David, for transit to the Atlantic. The Republic of Costa Rica has no outlet to the Atlantic; this little State is rapidly improving and for a long time has cast a longing eye towards Bocas del Toro; it is just what she wants: when the Road is constructed all her products and riches that now find their way to the Atlantic through the neigh-

boring State of Nicaragua, would by the nearer route
of David, be transported to Bocas del Toro; as also that
part now transmitted to Europe, via Cape Horn, which
would of course be diverted into the shorter channel.
Steamers would soon ply between David and San
Francisco, California; in fact the route across here
possesses so many solid advantages over all others yet
in contemplation, that the travelling public would as-
suredly adopt it in preference to any others.

J. WHITING, C. E.

NOVEMBER, 1851.

REPORT BY WILLIAM RIDLEY, Esq.,

CIVIL ENGINEER,

*On the Chiriqui route and Coal Formation Discovered
on the Pacific, near Costa Rica.*

The Passage by canoe from Panama to Rio Agua
Dulce was effected with a fair wind in about 36 hours.
From thence to Nata, distant about 8 miles, the beauty
of the scenery, the rich pasturage on the extensive
plains, the peculiar appearance of the ant-hills, eight
to nine feet in height, presenting at a distance the
appearance of a large encampment, the splendid
mineralogical specimens which on every side met my
view, and the presence of gold which is to be found
between the port Agua Dulce and Nata, presented

even at this short distance from Panama a striking
contrast to the Chagres route. Nata is a beautiful
and thriving city, present population about two thou-
sand. The magnificent altar of the church at this
place is of massive silver elaborately wrought, and of
immense value. * * * Early the following morn-
ing I started with a guide for the city of Santiago, the
Capital of the rich Province of Veraguas. The distance was stated to be 15 leagues, but it was certainly
the longest 45 miles I ever travelled. Tired and
weary, with a lame horse, grumbling guide, and a
dark night, I arrived at the city. No hotel was to be
found, and with some difficulty I procured lodgings for
myself and guide. The specimens of gold exhibited
to me by the Governor of Veraguas, Sen. Don Esco-
LASTICO ROMERO, as also an account of sales of an in-
voice of gold consigned to GLYNN & Co., Bankers,
London, the nett proceeds of which was equal to $17
the ounce, proved plainly the mineral wealth of the
province. Here I found large masses of gum caoutchouc.

The face of the country between Nata and Santiago is particularly level, until within 5 miles of the
latter city. From here until you reach the magnificent plains of La Mesa, you begin to experience mountain travel.

The Puebla of Los Remedios, commonly called
Puebla Nuevo, furnishes large supplies of the products
of the country to Panama and other places to the
eastward.

After a few miles on the road towards San Lorenzo
you again enter on the most magnificent plains I ever
beheld; perfectly level, they may be supposed to be

3

artificial rather than natural. These Campos, as they are called, particularly that of San Juan, with its picturesque haciendas and its immense herds of cattle and horses grazing on the luxuriant herbage, are unsurpassed in beauty and extent.

The artificial mounds in this vicinity cannot fail to attract the attention of the traveller. They are placed at regular distances, are very numerous, and undoubtedly contain aboriginal remains. Some of the rocks are covered with hieroglyphics.

The city of San Lorenzo is at present in ruins, and contains but few inhabitants; the distance thence to Chiriqui is about twelve leagues, the road crossing a range of mountains, but shortly entering the plains of David, which are of a similar description to those before mentioned. At Gualaca, and other parts of the Cordilleras, where a coal formation was represented to exist, I procured some fine specimens of the Orchidean family, specimens of the Espiritu Santo, some Oncidiums, and Octomeria, called by the natives Nina del Noche, emitting a delightful perfume, with numerous other valuable plants. In the higher regions of the Cordilleras, where the temperature is always cool and humid, others are to be found of rare beauty and value. From a point on the Sierra Bocas del Toro, both oceans are plainly visible. Specimens of native copper and copper ore with which the Cordilleras abound, were obtained in great variety.

The Puebla of David is superior in number and wealth of its inhabitants and in the peculiar advantages of its location to any other place on the Isthmus west of Panama. The port is three miles distant, and from the town to the Boquete Bocas del Toro is 18 miles, over a perfectly level country. From the Boquete (gap in the mountain) a wagon road across the Cordilleras has long been known to be practicable, the entire distance from Admiral's Bay on the Atlantic, to a port on the Pacific, both accessible to large vessels, is as nearly as possible 18 leagues. The vast mineral resources of this part of the Isthmus, the fertility of the plains, already cleared for miles to the hand of the agriculturist, the vegetable and botanical productions of luxuriant and spontaneous growth, the wide field open to the scientific traveller, the salubrity of the temperature, its contiguity to a port on the Atlantic, of easy access to the largest vessels, and with a port on the Pacific of equal commercial value, at both of which points, bituminous coal can be abundantly procured, must in a short time make this place, one of the greatest commercial cities on the Pacific.

Maize, coffee, tobacco, cotton, rice, yams, sweet potatoes, and all the tropical fruits, are produced spontaneously. The tea plant, canchalagua, sarsaparilla, senna, ginger, pepper, and hundreds of other valuable botanical and medicinal plants are abundant. The cedron, a specific for the bite of venomous insects and reptiles, is here to be procured; the pita, prepared from an agave, is superior in every respect to hemp; copaiva is used by the natives in lieu of oil for paint, and is found an admirable substitute. Dye-woods in every variety; gutta percha and caoutchouc, live oak of superior growth, and rosewood and mahogany, of the richest description, may be obtained at the cost of cutting and transportation.

The pearl fishery will afford another source of revenue, since native labor can readily be employed.

In the midst of these rich productions of nature, surrounded by groves of orange and lime trees, and generally on the banks of a navigable river, abounding with fish and shrimps of exquisite quality, the natives build their huts, caring not for the morrow. Deer, goats, game and wild fowl in great variety are readily procured by the bow and arrow, and turtle on the coast is abundant.

Cattle can readily be purchased at five dollars a head. In a few hôurs they can be driven into a temperature, in the mountain regions, where a fortune could be speedily realized, by packing beef and pork, for the Panama and other markets. Thousands of hogs run wild on the islands forming the Chiriqui Archipelago.

On an extensive peninsula, in the immediate vicinity of this groupe, (of Islands,) I succeeded in finding coal of such bituminous quality, and in such quantity as to realise every expectation. Reference to the Chart of the Coast, as surveyed two months since by the British sloop-of-war Herald, submitted with the specimens, will show the locality of the coal formation, as well as the advantages of shipment afforded by the harbor.

The coal, as proved on the spot, although an upper seam, and subject to the action of sea water for centuries, is highly bituminous, igniting freely at the flame of a candle, emitting a fierce flame and leaving little residuum. In this· respect it is fully equal to the upper seams of the best Newcastle or Scotch coals, which are generally considered superior for generating steam.

Of the quantity which can be procured, no doubt

can be entertained that it is sufficient to supply the steamers on the Pacific for ages, since I traced all the features and indications of a cóal deposit for miles in extent.

The expense of obtaining and shipping this coal will not, in my opinion exceed $30,000.

The copper ore found is of extraordinary quality. Several tons of ore was shipped on board the British sloop-of-war Herald, during the time she was engaged in the survey of the coast. &c., &c.

WM. W. RIDLEY,
CIVIL ENGINEER.

NEW YORK, 22d June, '49.

WHITING AND SHUMAN'S REPORT

UPON THE COAL FORMATION OF THE

ISLAND OF MUERTO.

This Island is situated in the Ensenada, or bay of the same name, about six hours sail from "Puerto Pedrigal" in the vicinity of David on the Pacific; it is about three miles long and one in breadth, rising high in the centre, well covered with fine, large, splendid timber, of various classes, suitable for building, among which are the Cedar, Mangle or Mangro. The island takes its name from the word "Dead," having a peculiar appearance as you approach it in a certain direction; in the centre there is a high mound, at the south east end there is another smaller, at the north west, another a little higher, these when seen from a certain point, have all the resemblance of a dead body laid out. From the monuments and columns found on the Island, it must have been used as a burial place of some ancient tribe of Indians, who inhabited the plains on the main land, in the vicinity. A gentleman resident of David, exhibited to us some large columns, taken from there; they are covered with hieroglyphics, not unlike those long hidden antiquities discovered by Stephens, in his researches and travels in Yucatan and Central America.

The landing place, is on the southern side, where a fine stream of water flows down from the hill, through a ravine close to the spot; the water is excellent, pure, sweet and abundant; the Island is easily approached; large vessels can reach it through "San Pedro" channel, and anchor close in, with perfect safety and facility; smaller vessels coming in from sea, through "Boca Chica," in the lower channel, pass very near the Island; the flood and ebb tides are every six hours; the average height is about from twelve to sixteen feet; the shore on all sides is bold, and some places quite high.

The most valuable feature in this Island, is the discovery of a highly bituminous *Coal Mine* on it. We dug out some from the surface, on the beach, which had been exposed to saline inundations for centuries. From such circumstances, we did not anticipate any thing worth the trouble of extracting, but to our agreeable surprise, it was found to be of excellent quality. The coal was taken from the surface; a fire was made of it, upon which we cooked our breakfast. We were astonished to see it burn so freely in its saturated state; it threw out a highly bituminous odour while burning, and left but little residuum. We had with us, a sample of the best English Coal, brought from Liverpool to Panama for the steamers there; we tried both, and found the Muerto Coal to burn equally as free as the other, emitting a bright, beautiful flame, with as much bitumem. The experiment we made of this coal, cannot but speak volumes in its favor, as the English Coal was of the very best, and the trial appeared to be in favor of the latter. Some people speak of this coal as being of a friable nature, it cannot be otherwise, being exposed to the action of the sea for ages; it must be taken into consideration, that this coal is taken from the upper strata, and not fair specimens to be compared with other coals. All miners are aware of the fact, that the upper strata, in every mine, at the commencement is of inferior quality. We venture to assert, that this coal is far superior to any yet found, without penetrating below the first formation. Where such favorable specimens are found upon the surface, there are great hopes certainly of procuring a better quality, when we come to the lower seams. This mine can be worked with great facility, the vein shooting upward in the adjoining bank. We traced coal on the opposite bank of the Island; we found pieces up in the ravine, which washed down from the heights by the rains, at some distance from where we found the first specimens.

The immediate vicinity of Panama, as a market for the coal, to supply all the California Steamers, the admirable position of the Island, so easy of access, closed in by an archipelago of Islands, rendering it safe from storms, or rough weather, the facility of mining the coal, the abundance of provisions, the cheapness of labor, all these requisites, so essential to render mining advantageous and lucrative to those engaged in it, cannot but make this island an object of great enterprise, and a valuable acquisition to those capitalists, who wish to make safe and profitable investments.

Another grand feature to render this island of immense value, is the road contemplated to be opened across this part of the Isthmus, being the shortest route over any part of it. The grant or right, has been ceded by the provincial authorities, in all due formality, in conformity to their laws, consequently, a market will be opened for the consumption of the coal on both sides, at the same time, without referring to distant places, for the sale of the commodity.

Signed,   JOHN WHITING,
A. B. SHUMAN.

David, April 1, 1851.

Analysis of Muerto Coal, carefully made by Professor Rogers of Pennsylvania, gives the following result,

Volatile and Butuminous parts,	36 27
Solid Carbon, - - -	58 48
Ashes, - - . - -	5 25
	100

It yields also in coke, 64 78 parts.

EXTRACTS

FROM

"THE MAHOGANY TREE,"

Published by Messrs. Chaloner & Fleming, Brokers,
Liverpool, 31*st. Dec.* 1850.

" The coasts of Veraguas and Costo Rica next deserve attention, for although no actual speculation is afloat to effect a passage
across there by canal or rails, still, as the American Isthmus
continues very narrow across there, and their shores both on the
Atlantic and Pacific, possess deeply indented bays and well
sheltered anchorages, these countries will very soon attract general attention from the richness of their productions, the fertility
of the soil, and quantity of virgin lands which are inviting to
the Colonist. The present governments of these provinces are
in the hands of persons who have avoided the intestine civil
wars, which have produced so much misery in the other parts
of the late Republic of Central America, and their enlightened
policy is reaping its reward in the rapid advancement of their
prosperity. In no part of the world are more encouragements
held out for colonists, and they will not be more than twenty
days sail from the markets on both sides of the Atlantic.

It has already been contemplated to effect a road from Bocas
del Toro to the gulf of Dulce in the Pacific; and when the
country is somewhat more advanced, there will be no great
obstacle to its execution, and that at no very distant day.

Attention is next directed to the countries on the Continent
of America, which are situated between the 8th and 13th de-
grees of North Latitude : and they are all comprised in what is

4

generally understood as the Isthmus, which connects the Continents of North and South America.

Comparatively with the vast extent of this immense Isthmus, the whole may be said to be little known to Europeans. Its surface is covered with the densest forests of mahogany, and other gigantic trees, with an underwood of many valuable tropical shrubs and plants, so matted together, that it is difficult for parties on foot to make a track into the interior.

The situation of this country is peculiarly favorable for commercial intercourse with every other part of the world; the whole of the great Pacific Ocean is before it to the West, and to the North and East it commands the Gulf of Mexico and the West Indies, and beyond them is the Atlantic Ocean, with Europe and Africa on one hand, and America on the other.

The soil of all these countries is, for the most part, exceedingly fertile. In the plains, and especially in the vallies, it is a dark rich mould, of alluvial formation, which might serve as manure for lands in other parts of the world. To this fertility of the soil, and to the gradations of temperature, may be attributed the variety and abundance of the productions, which embrace nearly all those of the West Indies, besides some that are peculiar to this country.

Of these the most valuable are Indigo, Cochineal, Tobacco, Cocoa, Vanilla and Wax; Sarsaparilla, Balsam of Peru, and the Amber Tree, Ginger, &c., which are staple commodities; Indian Corn, Rice, Yams, and Plantains, grow abundantly with little care. The Sugar-cane thrives luxuriantly, also the Coffee plant; and a species of cotton grows wild, which the Indians collect and manufacture into very beautiful fabrics. A great variety of Medicinal plants are collected, as well as Gums, Spices and Balsams, amongst which the most in esteem are the Copal, Acacia, Quitini, Quapinal, Incense, Chiracci, and the gum of the Chestnut Tree; and an oily substance is also extracted from the fruit of this tree, from which candles are made as fine as those of white wax. The fruits of this region are also incomparably fine, being of every kind to be found in the West Indies, and almost all European vegetables can be raised without any trouble.

But what is most important, and worthy of all attention in these parts, is the extent of its vast and interminable forests, replete with the most valuable timber trees already known to commerce, besides an infinite variety of Woods desirable for the Dyers, Cabinet Makers, House and Shipbuilders, the very names of which are scarcely known to Botanists, although the Indians have taken advantage of them for their primitive manufactures, and for the construction of their canoes and warlike instruments, esteeming them for their hardness, tenacity, elasticity or durability, according to their respective applications. Of the Dyewoods it is scarcely necessary to mention the Logwood, Fustic, Brazil Wood and Nicaragua, already so well known. The San Juan and the Poro yield a beautiful yellow, and the Ammona Reticulata, though perfectly white, changes colour on being cut or slit, and yields a clear brilliant red, which is easily extracted.

But the productions of the forest are those which, in the first instance, must fix particular attention in this publication, more especially, the trees of large growth.

The following are such as are already well known to the wood trade in this port, and admit of their qualities and uses being correctly appreciated. They are Oak, Ash, Beech, Cedar, Firs, Larches, Pitch Pines, Green Heart, Morra, Santa Maria, West India Teaks, Rosewood, Ebony, Satinwood, Sabicue, Lignumvitæ, Lancewood Spars, Maples, and Mahogany.

REPRESENTATION

*By the principal inhabitants of the town of. David, as
to the facilities and advantages of a road*

FROM THE ATLANTIC TO THE PACIFIC,

THROUGH THE PROVINCE OF CHIRIQUI BY

"BOCAS DEL TORO."

✓ The distance, from sea to sea at this point on the Isthmus,
that is to say, from Port Pedrigal on the Pacific, to the Lagoon
of Chiriqui, is from 17 to 20 leagues, and according to the information we have received, there is no doubt at all, but that a
carriage road can be opened from here to the said Lagoon of
Chiriqui on the Atlantic.

The mail between Carthagena and Bocas del Toro, passes
every month over this route. Droves of cattle and horses
traverse it with ease; from Pedrigal to the foot of the hills it is
almost a level, the ascent is so very gradual, with scarcely any
obstacles to be surmounted; this plain is in extent from 9 to 10
leagues, amongst the hills there may be from 7 to 8 leagues,
and on the other side 2 leagues more of plain, to the shores of
the Lagoon. It is said, and we know the fact, that throughout
this route, the rivers do not present obstacles of any difficulty,
being neither deep nor wide, bridges can be constructed across
them with great facility; on the banks are high bluffs on which
they can be based; during the heaviest freshet the water never
overflows them; the mountain gullies also are easily crossed,
either by bridges, or by making a circuit. With good engineers
and workmen accustomed to such work, we are persuaded that
every obstacle can be overcome with the greatest ease.

Having no means of making the calculation correctly, we cannot give the height of the Cordilleras, but we know very well that a road can be constructed through the passes without being carried over them. There are great abundance of woods of the largest dimensions, also stone and other materials. The climate on the Atlantic side is mild and temperate, fitted for the cultivation of the grains of the North, such as wheat, maize, barley, oats, &c., at the same time with those of the tropics; the seasons on the mountains are not so regular as in the plains, but variable, and resembling a more temperate climate; on the plains on the Pacific side, there is summer and winter; rice, tobacco, cotton, coffee, cocoa, maize, &c., are cultivated here; the fruits of the tropics also are plenty, such as the plantain, the orange, lime, breadfruit, &c.

The port of Bocas del Toro is the best in New Grenada, and without an equal in the world; that on the Pacific, commodious and excellent.

In the very short description which we here present, it is impossible to analyse all the advantages so satisfactory and appropriate for the construction of the said road, as are to be found in this province.

The country is healthy and very productive.

The natural advantages and facilities innumerable.

The provincial government and the entire population, are very greatly in favor of the undertaking. Labor and provisions are very cheap, workmen can be had for 3 or 4 rials per day, (37½ to 50 cents.)

Our judgment and opinion are very much in favor of said road and enterprise, and we will give prompt and decided assistance, so far as in our power, for the completion of a work so essential to the prosperity of this country.

ANGEL FRANCESCHI,   JN. MANUEL LOPEZ,
JN. MIGL. LABARRIERE,   S. MONTECALTINI,
JN. BASTINO JARADA,   R. MACDOWALL, M. D.

David, April 5th, 1851.

I certify by these presents, that I, Jose Maria Condenedo, Alcalde of the parrochial district of the town of David, know the gentlemen whose signatures to the above document are attached, and that the information that is given therein, is correct, and worthy of all confidence, they being of the most respectable and intelligent inhabitants of this town.

    (Signed,)   JOSE MARIA CONDENEDO.

David, April 5th, 1851.

Government House, Province of Fabrega :

I certify that Jose Maria Condenedo, who signs the preceding certificate, is Alcalde of the parrochial district of David.

    (Signed,)   PABLO AROSEMENA.

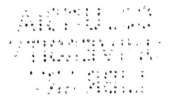

Lightning Source UK Ltd.
Milton Keynes UK
UKHW020639260922
409457UK00005B/455